P9-APH-522

To a Wonderful Teacher

_____

_____

_____

a Teacher

affects eternity

ANDREWS AND MCMEEL

A Universal Press Syndicate Company

KANSAS CITY

A Teacher Affects Eternity copyright © 1995 by Smallwood and Stewart, Inc. All rights reserved. Printed in Singapore. No part of this book may be used or reproduced in any manner whatsoever without written permission except in the case of reprints in context of reviews. For information, write Andrews and McMeel, a Universal Press Syndicate Company, 4900 Main Street, Kansas City, Missouri 64112.

ISBN: 0-8362-4246-7

Library of Congress Catalog Card Number: 94-73313

Printed in Singapore

First U.S. edition

1 3 5 7 9 10 8 6 4 2

Edited by Linda Sunshine

Designed by Pat Tan

Produced by Smallwood and Stewart, Inc.,
New York City

Notice: Every effort has been made to locate the copyright owners of the material used in the book. Please let us know if an error has been made, and we will make any necessary changes in subsequent printings.

Credits and copyright notices appear on pages 94–95

In a recent *New York Times* article, Stephen Sondheim, the renowned composer and lyricist, spoke to an interviewer about his early teachers—Oscar Hammerstein, Robert Barrow at Williams College and the avant-garde composer Milton Babbitt. "I hear the word teacher and I start to get teary," Sondheim reported. "The word 'teacher' is that thing that—for religious people—God and saints are."

Reading this article reminded me that many of us regard our teachers in such a light, for a truly great teacher does much more than educate. He or she can profoundly affect, and direct, the course of a life. And such a monumental achievement often goes unacknowledged. Sometimes we take our teachers for granted; other times, years may pass before we realize a teacher's contribution to our lives. In either case, this book is meant to counter such an oversight, for it is filled with remembrances and accolades from such gifted writers as Thomas Wolfe, Annie Dillard, Eudora Welty, Conrad Aiken, E. B. White, Jessamyn West, Beryl Markham, and many others; all of whom have written so eloquently about teachers and the teaching profession.

Personally, I have been blessed with three great teachers in my life. In fifth grade, Mr. Hall used to sing through the alphabet and tap dance the names of the capitols. He showed me that education could be entertaining. Mrs. Urquhart, in eleventh grade, believed that I could write and often selected my essays to read aloud to the class. And, much later, when I was in my thirties, an Englishman named Robin taught me how to horseback ride. His first lessons concerned how to fall off a horse without getting hurt and, from Robin, I learned not only how to jump fences but, also, how to confront my fears.

No matter what the subject, teaching is an extraordinary profession which can carry its rewards down through generations—for we teach our children what was taught to us.

Thus, we lovingly dedicate this book to all those who teach but, most particularly, to that special teacher who received this book from a grateful student. Thank you for a job well done.

LINDA SUNSHINE

It is the supreme art of the teacher

to awaken joy in creative expression

and knowledge. ALBERT EINSTEIN

It was from this house that my mother very soon after that piled up her hair and went out to teach in a one-room school, mountain children little and big alike. The first day, some fathers came along to see if she could whip their children, some who were older than she. She told the children that she did intend to whip them if they became unruly and refused to learn, and invited the fathers to stay if they liked and she'd be able to whip them too. Having been thus tried out, she was a great success with them after that. She left home every day on her horse; since she had the river to cross, a little brother rode on her horse behind her, to ride him home, while she rowed across the river in a boat. And he would be there to meet her with her horse again at evening. All this way, to pass the time, she told me, she recited the poems in McGuffey's Readers out loud.

She could still recite them in full when she was lying helpless and nearly blind, in her bed, an old lady. Reciting, her voice took on resonance and firmness, it rang with the old fervor, with ferocity even. She was teaching me one more, almost her last, lesson: emotions do not grow old. I knew that I would feel as she did, and I do.

EUDORA WELTY
One Writer's Beginnings

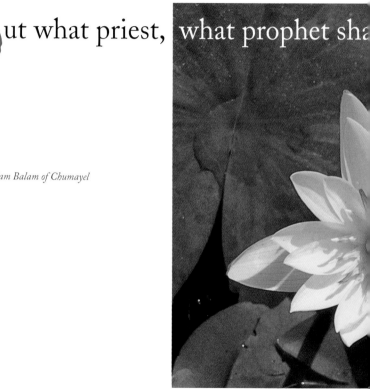

But what priest, what prophet sha

The Book of Chilam Balam of Chumayel

xplain the words of the books . . . ?

[Mary Wollstonecraft Shelley] was choosing a school for her son, and asked the advice of this lady, who gave for advice—to use her own words to me— 'Just the sort of banality, you know, one does come out with: "Oh, send him somewhere where they will teach him to think for himself!" ' . . . Mrs Shelley answered: 'Teach him to think for himself? Oh, my God, teach him rather to think like other people!'

MATTHEW ARNOLD

Is it a cow?

It is a cow.

It is my cow.

She has no hay.

Let her be fed.

McGuffey's Pictorial Eclectic Primer

For some reason the sight of them frightens me slightly.

I'm used to teaching grown-ups.

ALEXANDER SOLZHENITSYN
"For the Good of the Cause"

What sculpture is to a block of marble,
education is to the soul.

J O S E P H   A D D I S O N

The Avonlea school was a whitewashed

building low in the eaves and wide in the

windows, furnished inside with comfortable

substantial old-fashioned desks that opened

and shut, and were carved all over their

lids with the initials and hieroglyphics of

three generations of schoolchildren. The

schoolhouse was set back from the road and

behind it was a dusky fir wood and a brook

where all the children put their bottles of

milk in the morning to keep cool and sweet

until dinner hour.

L. M. MONTGOMERY
Anne of Green Gables

But I follow her from Spelling,

    with her hand behind her—so—

And I slip the apple in it—

    and the Teacher doesn't know!

JAMES WHITCOMB RILEY
An Old Sweetheart of Mine

He read quickly and easily; he spelled accurately. He did well with figures. But he hated the drawing lesson, although the boxes of crayons and paints delighted him. Sometimes the class would go into the woods, returning with specimens of flowers and leaves—the bitten flaming red of the maple, the brown pine comb, the brown oak leaf. These they would paint; or in Spring a spray of cherry-blossom, a tulip. He sat reverently before the authority of the plump woman who first taught him: he was terrified lest he do anything common or mean in her eyes.

THOMAS WOLFE
Look Homeward, Angel

uch of what I believe about teaching can be found in the story the pianist Claudio Arrau tells about his early years. "The first two teachers in Berlin were boring," he told an interviewer. "I wanted only to read more music, to perform more music. At 8, I loved the piano so, I would take my meals at the keyboard. By 10, dull teaching had turned me against music and myself."

"But you were rescued," the interviewer said.

"Desperate at 10," Arrau continued, "I was taken to play for Martin Krause. He was a severe old man, but children feel reality and behind the harsh mask was an incredible gift for opening up worlds."

Few teachers can have pupils like Arrau, but all teachers have the opportunity for opening up worlds.

KENNETH E. EBLE
The Craft of Teaching

A teacher affects eternity; he car

ever tell where his influence stops.

HENRY B. ADAMS

And what I have always thought was the real turning point of my life came one day when, in the small class-room, after an expression of aggrieved disappointment in our work, she turned, looked at me and said, "I think *Conrad* will someday amount to something."

This accolade changed my life in an instant. It gave me the self-belief and courage which I hadn't hitherto had, and a purpose and center, too. Who can possibly weigh the consequences of such an action? Incalculable, at any rate, they were for me, and it grieves me that I was never able to tell her so. It was more than thirty years before I was to return to Savannah, and by then she was many years dead. But I could tell her children and grand-children, I am happy to say.

CONRAD AIKEN
Four Teachers

We knelt over the pool.

We saw the anemones opening

to welcome the incoming tide;

we saw the crayfish lurking

ominously in their caves.

THORNTON WILDER
Theophilus North

This year at the Ellis School my sister Amy was in the fifth grade, with Mrs. McVicker. I remembered Mrs. McVicker fondly. Every year she reiterated the familiar (and, without a description of their mechanisms, the sentimental) mysteries that schoolchildren hear so often and so indifferently: that each snowflake is different, that some birds fly long distances, that acorns grow into oaks. Caterpillars turn into butterflies. The stars are large and very far away. She struck herself like a gong with these same mallets every year—a sweet old schoolteacher whom we in our time had loved and tolerated for her innocence.

ANNIE DILLARD
An American Childhood

Girls scream,

Boys shout;

Dogs bark,

School's out.

W. H. DAVIES
School's Out

One looks back with appreciation to the brilliant teachers, but with gratitude to those who touched our human feelings. The curriculum is so much necessary raw material, but the warmth is the vital element for the growing plant and for the soul of

A good education should leave much to be desired.

ALAN GREGG

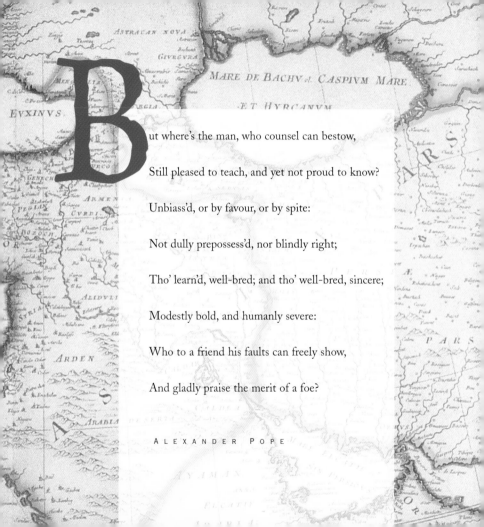

But where's the man, who counsel can bestow,

Still pleased to teach, and yet not proud to know?

Unbiass'd, or by favour, or by spite:

Not dully prepossess'd, nor blindly right;

Tho' learn'd, well-bred; and tho' well-bred, sincere;

Modestly bold, and humanly severe:

Who to a friend his faults can freely show,

And gladly praise the merit of a foe?

ALEXANDER POPE

And why," I asked myself, "why should I have learned that this precious book exists, if I am never to possess it—never even to see it? I would go to seek it in the burning heart of Africa, or in the icy regions of the Pole if I knew it were there. But I do not know where it is. I do not know if it be guarded in a triple-locked iron case by some jealous bibliomaniac. I do not know it if be growing mouldy in the attic of some ignoramus. I shudder at the thought that perhaps its torn-out leaves may have been used to cover the pickle-jars of some housekeeper."

ANATOLE FRANCE
The Crime of Sylvestre Bonnard

Come forth into the light of things,

L

et Nature be your teacher.

WILLIAM WORDSWORTH

Education is not th

lling of a pail, but the lighting of a fire.

WILLIAM BUTLER YEATS

We began at the first hour of the morning. We began when the sky was clean and ready for the sun and you could see your breath and smell traces of the night. We began every morning at that same hour, using what we were pleased to call the Nairobi Aerodrome, climbing away from it with derisive clamour, while the burghers of the town twitched in their beds and dreamed perhaps of all unpleasant things that drone—of wings and stings, and corridors in Bedlam.

Tom taught me in a D. H. Gipsy Moth, at first, and her propeller beat the sunrise silence of the Athi Plains to shreds and scraps. We swung over the hills and over the town and back again, and I saw how a man can be master of a craft, and how a craft can be master of an element. I saw the alchemy of perspective reduce my world, and all my other life, to grains in a cup. I learned to watch, to put my trust in other hands than mine. And I learned to wander. I learned what every dreaming child needs to know—that no horizon is so far that you cannot get above it or beyond it. These I learned at once. But most things came harder.

Tom Black had never taught another soul to fly, and the things he had to teach beyond the simple mechanics that go with flying are those things that have not lent themselves to words. Intuition and instinct are mysteries still. . . .

BERYL MARKHAM
West With the Night

I had a terrible education. I attended school

for emotionally disturbed teachers.

WOODY ALLEN

I was fifteen and my teacher may have been in his early twenties, a poet who gave us the beauty of listening to and reading poetry that throbbed and sang. There was such test of meaning that it was a living experience which would continue to give its glow and its beauty to the whole of our lives.

Did I ever say "thank you" to him, you ask? Not really, unless this can be considered a "thank you" long, long after the happening. But that class came eager to its room, was attentive and participating, a most responsive group, and all this must have given him a sense that he was reaching the people he was teaching. That in itself must have been his reward.

CAROLINE K. SIMON
A Remembered Glow

The first duty of a lecturer—to hand you after an hour's discourse a nugget of pure truth to wrap up between the pages of your notebooks and keep on the mantelpiece for ever.

VIRGINIA WOOLF

I had taught at Liberty School for six years and I loved that place. It was "beautiful for situation" as the Bible says, located ten miles out of town in the rolling semi-dry upland country where the crop was grain, not apricots and peaches. It was a one-room school, and I was its only teacher. . . . Kids learned to read there. At the end of the sixth year there was only one eighth grader who could beat me in mental arithmetic. I was the acknowledged champion at skin-the-cat and could play adequately any position on the softball team.

JESSAMYN WEST
The Condemned Librarian

There was one in grammar school, there was one in high school, and there was one in college. All three, I now perceive, were possessed of spirit, and it was the spirit, not the mind, that distinguished them from other teachers. I feel in their debt. School is not an easy time for most scholars who, like mariners, are always on the lookout for some aid to navigation.

E. B. WHITE
Trinity

Creative teachers are creative because they have kept in touch with their own hidden sources of emotional energy. If you are to remain an alert teacher, you must not only live for the class; otherwise the level of your consciousness will drop to that of the class and you will then become a companion rather than a guide. You must continue to be an intellectual adventurer, quick to pitch tent on the fluctuating boundaries of the known. You must continue to develop and refine your own talent.

PETER ABBS

I remember when there was no gas or electric light and we used to have a member of the domestic staff called a lamp-boy—he did nothing else but clean and trim and light lamps throughout the School. I remember when there was a hard frost that lasted for seven weeks in the winter term—there were no games, and the whole School learned to skate on the fens. Eighteen-eighty-something, that was. . . . I remember . . . I remember . . . but chiefly I remember all your faces. I never forget them. I have thousands of faces in my mind—the faces of boys. If you come and see me again in the years to come—as I hope you all will—I shall try to remember those older faces of yours, but it's just possible that I shan't be able to—and then some day you'll see me somewhere and I shan't recognize you and you'll say to yourself, 'The old boy doesn't remember me.' [Laughter] But I *do* remember you—as you are *now*. That's the point. In my mind you never grow up at all. Never.

JAMES HILTON
Good-bye, Mr. Chips

The teacher should never lose his temper in the presence of the class. If a man, he may take refuge in profane soliloquies; if a woman, she may follow the example of one sweet-faced and apparently tranquil girl—go out in the yard and gnaw a post.

WILLIAM LYON PHELPS

He and some one hundred and forty schoolmasters had been lately turned at the same time in the same factory, on the same principles, like so many pianoforte legs. He had been put through an immense variety of paces, and had answered volumes of head-breaking questions. Orthography, etymology, syntax and prosody, biography, astronomy, geography and general cosmography, the sciences of compound proportion, algebra, land surveying and levelling, vocal music and drawing from models, were all at the ends of his ten chilled fingers. He had worked his stony way into Her Majesty's most Honourable Privy Counsil's Schedule B, and had taken the bloom off the higher branches of mathematics and physical science, French, German, Latin and Greek. He knew all about all the Water sheds of all the world (whatever they are) and all the histories of all the peoples and all the names of all the rivers and mountains, and all the productions, manners and customs of all the countries, and all their boundaries and bearings on the two and thirty points of the compass. Ah, rather overdone, M'Choakumchild. If he had only learnt a little less, how infinitely better he might have taught much more!

CHARLES DICKENS
Hard Times

Teachers have played a great part in my life. I owe them so much that I have tried to repay part of my indebtedness by doing, I believe and hope, what would please than most—by being a teacher myself. When trying to teach, I always had them in mind.

REGINALD HEBER SMITH
A Career Is Born

Go and catch a falling star,

Get with child a mandrake root,

Tell me where all past years are,

Or who cleft the devil's foot;

Teach me to hear mermaids singing

And find

What wind

Serves to advance an honest mind.

JOHN DONNE

a falling star

Between the sarcasms and the

ironies, occasional smiles, the rare

warm reading of a line or two, an

aesthetic sense leaked through.

ROBERT MACNEIL

I was an obedient student, if anything a little oversold on the possibilities of this bounteous institution called school.

JOHN UPDIKE
Self-Consciousness

If it were not that the average

public school teacher has given the public much more

than he has received, it would have gone hard with the

schools and education in our country.

Report on the Educational System of South Dakota, 1918, Department of Interior, Bureau of Education

Headmasters have powers at their disposal with

which Prime Ministers have never yet been invested.

WINSTON CHURCHILL

I don't remember being frightened or unfrightened by school. My mother, who had never played me false before, simply took me by the hand one morning and walked me three blocks down the street. Suddenly, I was alone in the middle of a large chunk of stone, inhaling chalk dust, staring at a row of scissors winking in the sun, and watching Miss Burdette tug with a long, hooked, wooden pole at the upper windows, which gave out onto the cement playground beyond. With one clap of the erasers I had moved into another dimension. School was something larger and more meaningful than myself.

PHYLLIS THEROUX
California and Other States of Grace

My teacher told me today was the first day of the rest of my life. That explains why I didn't do yesterday's homework.

LORNE ELLIOT

To see a world in a

And a Heaven in a

Hold Infinity in the

And Eternity in an

grain of sand

wild flower,

palm of your hand,

hour.

WILLIAM BLAKE

It is in fact a part of the function of education to help us escape—not from our own time, for we are bound by that—but from the intellectual and emotional limitations of our own time.

T. S. ELIOT

A C K N O W L E D G M E N T S

Peter Abbs quotation reprinted by permission of the publisher from Bolin, Frances & Falk, Judith McConnell, *Teacher Renewal.* (New York: Teachers College Press, copyright © 1987 by Teachers College, Columbia University. All rights reserved.)

Excerpt from "Four Teachers" by Conrad Aiken from *The Teacher* edited by Morris L. Ernst. Copyright © 1967 by Morris L. Ernst. Used by permission of the publisher, Prentice Hall/a Division of Simon & Schuster.

Bureau of Education quotation reprinted by permission of the publisher from Bolin, Frances & Falk, Judith McConnell, *Teacher Renewal.* (New York: Teachers College Press, copyright © 1987 by Teachers College, Columbia University. All rights reserved.

Excerpt from *An American Childhood* by Annie Dillard. Copyright © 1987 by Annie Dillard. Reprinted by permission of HarperCollins Publishers, Inc.

Excerpt from *Goodbye, Mr. Chips* by James Hilton. Copyright 1934 by James Hilton; © 1962 by Alice Hilton. By permission of Little, Brown and Company.

Excerpt from "Birth of a Life" from *West With the Night* by Beryl Markham. Copyright © 1942, 1983 by Beryl Markham. Reprinted by permision of North Point Press, a division of Farrar, Straus & Giroux, Inc.

Excerpt from "A Remembered Glow" by Caroline K. Simon from *The Teacher* edited by Morris L. Ernst. Copyright © 1967 by Morris L. Ernst. Used by permission of the publisher, Prentice Hall/a Division of Simon & Schuster.

Excerpt from *California and Other States of Grace* by Phyllis Theroux, copyright © 1980 by Phyllis Theroux, reprinted by permission of William Morrow and Company, Inc.

Excerpt from *One Writer's Beginnings* by Eudora Welty, copyright © 1983, 1984 by Eudora Welty, reprinted by permission of Harvard University Press.

Excerpt from "The Condemned Librarian" in *Crimson Ramblers of the World, Farewell,* copyright © 1970 by Jessamyn West, reprinted by permission of Harcourt Brace & Company.

Excerpt from "Trinity" by E. B. White from *The Teacher* edited by Morris L. Ernst. Copyright © 1967 by Morris L. Ernst. Used by permission of the publisher, Prentice Hall/a Division of Simon & Schuster.

Excerpt from *Look Homeward, Angel* by Thomas Wolfe reprinted with permission of Charles Scribner's Sons, an imprint of Macmillan Publishing, copyright 1929 Charles Scribner's Sons; copyright renewed © 1957 Edward C. Aswell, as Administrator, C.T.A. of the Estate of Thomas Wolfe and/or Fred W. Wolfe.

Other attributions as follows: Henry Brooks Adams from his *Education of Henry Adams,* Mathew Arnold, from his *Essays in Criticism, Second Series: Shelley;* T. S. Eliot from his obituary in *The New York Times,* January 5, 1965; William Lyon Phelps from his *Teaching in School and College;* Alexander Pope from *An Essay on Criticism.*

ART CREDITS

Courtesy of: Archive Photos–Harold Lambert: 44, 56, 86; Envision–Jack Stein Grove: 38; e. t. Archive: 5; FPG International–Carol Graham: 20, Spencer Grant: 81, Keystone View Co: 9, 34; The Image Bank–Peter Fiore: 96, Robert Kristofik: 77, Wm. A. Logan: 67, Linda Montgomery: 88, Obremski: 10, Erik Leigh Simmons: 24, Jeff Spielman: 49, Pete Turner: 62; Lynn Karlin: 52, 64, 68; Andrew Lawson: 15, 32, 33, 50, 74; The Metropolitan Museum of Art–Robert Lehman Collection, 1975, Pierre Auguste Renoir *Two Young Girls at the Piano* (1975.1.201): 30, The Metropolitan Museum of Art–Gift of Louise Senff Cameron in memory of Charles H. Senff, 1928, Jean Baptiste Corot *A Woman Reading* (28.90): 93; Monica Roberts: 42; Susan Sternau: 58; Superstock–Winslow Homer *Snap the Whip*: 41, 61; Jonathan Wallen: 23; Mary Watkins: 70, endpapers. Handmade paper backgrounds created by Matthew Carman.